THE ARCHITECTURE
—— OF ——
WEALTH

*A Complete Metaphysical System for
Manifesting, Retaining, and Circulating Power*

Copyright © 2025 by Ancient The Architect
All rights reserved.
Published by Health Is Luxury LLC

No part of this book may be copied, reproduced, stored, or transmitted in any form or by any means—electronic, mechanical, photocopying, recording, or otherwise—without prior written permission from the publisher, except in the case of brief quotations embodied in critical articles, reviews, or teachings with proper attribution.

This book is a work of metaphysical philosophy. It is intended for educational and spiritual development purposes only. The author makes no claims regarding specific financial or psychological outcomes. The reader assumes full responsibility for how they interpret and apply the material within.

ISBN: 979-8-9922102-6-2
Printed in the United States of America
First Edition – 2025

Cover Design © 2025 by Ancient The Architect
Interior Layout by Health Is Luxury LLC
www.HealthIsLuxury.org

THE ARCHITECTURE
— OF —
WEALTH

*A Complete Metaphysical System for
Manifesting, Retaining, and Circulating Power*

By Ancient The Architect

*To those who remember that wealth
is not earned—it is permitted.
To the architects of reality who know that
frequency is the true currency.
To those reclaiming their birthright of
Frequency Capital—stored not in banks,
but in the causal body.*

Table of Contents

- *Lecture I: Belief Over Desire*
- *Lecture II: The Four Inner Bodies of Wealth*
- *Lecture III: Soul Contracts & Ancestral Codes*
- *Lecture IV: Causal Treasuries & Spiritual Assets*
- *Lecture V: Collapsing the Timeline of Delay*
- *Lecture VI: Resonant Return & Energetic Exchange*
- *Lecture VII: Field Sovereignty and Sealing Power*
- *Advanced I: Wealth as Weapon*
- *Advanced II: The Alchemy of Circulation*
- *Advanced III: The Geometry of Divine Compensation*
- *Final Benediction: The Seal of Sovereign Wealth*

Introduction

This is not a book about money.
This is a book about **power, architecture, and field design**.

The Architecture of Wealth is a metaphysical transmission—an encoded system of lectures that dismantles every illusion you've been taught about how wealth is created, received, and retained. It bypasses the surface-level affirmations, the tired manifestation rhetoric, and the guilt-laced spiritual scarcity codes. Instead, it delivers a complete structural blueprint—layer by layer—for how wealth actually moves through the subtle bodies, karmic fields, and belief architectures of consciousness.

This book does not teach you how to chase abundance.
It shows you how to **become the sovereign frequency that wealth cannot ignore**.

THE ARCHITECTURE OF WEALTH – LECTURE I

The Metaphysical Mechanics of Manifestation

1. Wealth as a Field, Not a Possession

Wealth is not an object.
It is not the paper you trade, the metals you hoard, or the accounts you track.
Wealth is a **frequency field**—a resonant structure of **conscious permission**.

At the metaphysical level, wealth is not *something you get*—
It is *something your field allows*.

You allow it by sustaining a **harmonic** between your inner cognition and the frequency of resource.
If there is a mismatch—if even one fracture of guilt, doubt, or spiritual distortion exists—you unconsciously collapse the field that permits wealth to enter.

2. Belief Is the Substrate of Reality

Desire is electrical—it moves quickly but dies without grounding.
Belief is magnetic—it pulls reality toward it with gravitational density.

You do not manifest what you want.
You manifest what your field can hold.
And your field can only hold what your **subtle body believes is real**.

Belief is not intellectual agreement.
Belief is the **energetic permission slip** stored in the layers of your causal body, shaped by inherited systems, karmic agreements, early imprints, and subtle spiritual contracts.

Until these contracts are rewritten, no external effort will override the structure of your manifestation grid.

3. The Gap Between Desire and Belief: The Root of Misalignment

The distance between what you say you want and what you actually allow is not psychological.

It is metaphysical. It is the gap between two energy signatures:

- **Desire**: the outer symbol
- **Belief**: the inner architecture

This gap is occupied by **thought-forms**—subconscious entities that act like security gates. They regulate the inflow of energy based on your soul's programming.

If you believe wealth makes people arrogant...
If you associate abundance with exploitation or stress...
Your thought-forms will sabotage manifestation to protect your identity structure.

This sabotage isn't negative—it is loyal. Your system is simply refusing to manifest what you have labeled as *unsafe*.

4. The First Task: Audit Your Inner Field

The path begins not with goal setting, but with **energetic inventory**.

Ask:

- What do I believe wealth will do to me?
- What early events defined my relationship with money?
- Whose voice lives inside my idea of wealth?
- Do I perceive wealth as responsibility, risk, or power?

You must locate the **origin signatures** of your field distortions.
Where the thought-forms were born.
Where the belief patterns took root.

Only then can you reprogram the structure.

THE ARCHITECTURE OF WEALTH – LECTURE II

The Four Types of Inner Wealth & the Bodies That Govern Them

In this transmission, we step beyond general ideas of wealth and define its **anatomy**.
There is not one form of wealth—but four.
And each one is governed by a different **subtle body** within your system.

To attract holistic wealth, all four must be brought into alignment.
Any one body out of sync becomes a fracture point—where opportunity leaks, momentum stalls, or manifestation breaks down.

1. Vital Wealth – Governed by the Physical Body

This is the wealth of **vital energy**—your biological capacity to move, build, respond, and take action.
It is not just health. It is *aliveness*.
It manifests as strength, immunity, stamina,

and the ability to handle high-frequency transformation without collapse.

Without vital wealth, even great ideas die in inertia.
You may visualize endlessly, but if your biology lacks vitality, the body will resist expansion.

Symptoms of deficiency: fatigue, illness, procrastination, shallow breath, fear of action.

Correction: Breathwork, sun exposure, sleep regulation, and grounding nutrition— **vital repair awakens the first gate of wealth.**

2. Mental Wealth – Governed by the Lower Mind (Manas)

Mental wealth is your **thought structure** —the inner atmosphere of your decisions and focus.

A wealthy mind has precision, clarity, silence, and direction.
A poor mind loops, wanders, reacts, and collapses under complexity.

Mental wealth determines how you **organize time**, **perceive challenges**, and **interpret failure**.

Symptoms of deficiency: overthinking, mental fog, chronic indecision, anxiety around money or performance.

Correction: Remove mental clutter. Design conscious thought-forms. Audit and eliminate inherited mental poverty patterns from family, religion, and media.

3. Emotional Wealth – Governed by the Astral Body

Emotional wealth is your **capacity to hold frequency under pressure.**
It's not about how you feel—
It's about how much charge your field can contain without distortion.

A person with emotional wealth can **withstand abundance** without sabotage. They can receive without guilt. Hold power without collapse. Remain centered when tested.

Symptoms of deficiency: jealousy, guilt, comparison, guilt-driven giving, emotional avoidance, or cycles of feast and famine.

Correction: Deconstruct internal conflict. Practice emotional non-reactivity. Build emotional bandwidth to *receive without distortion.*

4. Causal Wealth – Governed by the Higher Self

This is the **master key** of wealth.
Causal wealth is your stored **karmic credit and soul inheritance**—
The inner light that permits high-frequency attraction.

You do not create causal wealth through work.
You **unlock it** through alignment.

When you function in your higher archetype, in harmony with your soul code, causal wealth activates as **effortless synchronicity**—opportunities, connections, and resources magnetize toward you with no linear explanation.

Symptoms of deficiency: blocked intuition, random self-sabotage, sudden collapse after success, or unexplained misfortune.

Correction: Soul alignment. Fulfill the inner contract. Honor the design you came here with. **Causal wealth requires obedience to your highest frequency.**

Summary: The Wealth Quadrant

- **Vital Wealth** – Energy & Action – *Physical Body*

- **Mental Wealth** – Thought Structure – *Lower Mind*

- **Emotional Wealth** – Frequency Holding – *Astral Body*

- **Causal Wealth** – Soul Inheritance – *Higher Self*

All four must be active and harmonized. When one collapses, all others begin to leak.

This is why people who "work hard" often remain poor.
They may be rich in **vital wealth** but

bankrupt in **causal wealth**.
Or those who "think positively" but are weighed down by emotional sabotage.

Wealth is not a goal.
It is the natural result of energetic integration.

THE ARCHITECTURE OF WEALTH – LECTURE III

Soul Contracts, Ancestral Patterns & the Inheritance of Poverty Codes

Wealth is not simply personal.
It is **ancestral**.
It is **karmic**.
It is **contractual**.

Before you ever touched currency, your field was already shaped by forces larger than this life—by contracts you didn't consciously sign, but were encoded into your system through **lineage**, **culture**, and **unfinished karmic loops**.

These are not metaphors. They are energetic realities that govern the **flow permissions** of your subtle system.

1. What Is a Soul Contract?

A soul contract is an **agreement made in the causal plane**—either by you or your lineage—to accept certain limitations or roles as part of an evolutionary cycle.

These can look like:

- "I will never be like my father."
- "I must suffer to be spiritual."
- "We don't talk about money in our family."
- "We survive through struggle."
- "Our people have always been poor."

These phrases are more than beliefs. They are **energy signatures**—and once embedded, they govern your field like spiritual code.

Until these contracts are revoked or rewritten, they act as **invisible ceilings**—no matter how much effort you apply, your field hits a barrier it can't override.

2. Ancestral Poverty Codes

Poverty is often romanticized.
It's framed as humble, spiritual, or pure.
But this is a weaponized distortion—
implanted through centuries of trauma, colonization, and suppression.

Many spiritual traditions were **infiltrated by life-negative programming** that elevated poverty and demonized prosperity.

The result?

Entire lineages that **equate lack with goodness**.

This becomes an inherited frequency—passed not just through words, but through emotional imprinting, nervous system regulation, and unresolved grief.

If you grew up hearing "money is the root of all evil"...
If your elders suffered silently, and suffering was normalized...
Then wealth may feel like betrayal.

Even when you desire wealth, your subconscious holds loyalty to the poverty of your lineage. That loyalty creates an inner split.

3. Karmic Loops & Field Entanglement

Some contracts were not created in this lifetime.

You may be carrying **karmic debris** from lives where wealth led to your downfall...
Or where abundance was used for manipulation, greed, or betrayal.

These karmic imprints create a **field-level entanglement**—you unconsciously sabotage your wealth because you associate it with guilt or danger.

And so, every time wealth gets close...
You energetically **repel** it to stay safe.

This is why success can feel triggering.
Why abundance brings anxiety.
Why sabotage happens right before the breakthrough.

It is not personal. It is **patterned**.

4. Clearing Contracts and Energetic Debts

To clear these contracts, you must first become aware of them.

Ask yourself:

- Who in my family feared money?

- What spiritual vows may I still be carrying?
- When do I feel unworthy to receive?
- What patterns repeat in my financial life?

Then declare:

"I revoke all energetic contracts that bind me to lack, guilt, and survival."
"I release ancestral patterns that define wealth as dangerous or impure."
"I reclaim my field. I choose wealth as a tool of higher service and evolution."

This is not just affirmation.
This is **field reprogramming**.

THE ARCHITECTURE OF WEALTH – LECTURE IV

Spiritual Assets & the Causal Body's Hidden Treasury

In this transmission, we decode one of the most advanced metaphysical principles of wealth:

Not all wealth is created. Some wealth is remembered.

There is a treasury hidden in the deeper folds of your being—stored not in your mind, your bank, or your goals—but in the **causal body**.
This treasury is not made of gold, but of **energetic authority**.
It is your original soul inheritance.
Not earned. Not deserved. Simply latent.
Waiting for access.

1. What Are Spiritual Assets?

Spiritual assets are not currency.
They are not stocks or properties.

They are **field permissions**—subtle frequencies your soul carries across lifetimes.
They determine how reality organizes itself around you.

Examples of spiritual assets:

- Natural magnetism (charisma, draw)
- Instant manifestation ability
- Intuitive timing
- High-value aura (others sense opportunity through you)
- Abundance codes in your voice, presence, or frequency
- Ease with receiving without guilt or contraction

These are not taught. They are carried.

Just as some people are born with a physical inheritance, others are born with **causal access to wealth fields**—spiritual permission to attract and hold abundance, effortlessly.

2. Why Some People Magnetize Wealth Without Effort

This is not luck.
This is **causal alignment**.

Their soul has either:

- Already transcended the poverty contract in a prior life

- Carried over a surplus of completed dharma

- Or is operating from a timeline where wealth is aligned with their soul's mission

These people are not better.
They are simply broadcasting from a **different layer of the grid**.

They do not manifest wealth.
Wealth **orients around them** as a field response.

This is what many confuse as "privilege" or "fate."
But in truth, it is **stored karma**, activated through field readiness.

3. Dormant Treasuries: Unlocking What You Already Carry

The great tragedy is not that people lack wealth.
It is that they carry massive treasuries **locked behind false identities**.

If you grew up in scarcity, surrounded by lack-based thinking, guilt, or religious suppression—your spiritual assets may still be present, but **dormant**.

They are wrapped in protective belief systems that were designed to keep you safe—but now keep you small.

To activate these treasuries, you must:

- Disidentify from inherited narratives of "just enough"

- Revoke unconscious vows of poverty, sacrifice, or invisibility

- Align with your higher archetype—the soul role that permits access to abundance as a natural extension of who you are

Wealth then becomes not a goal, but a **function of authenticity**.

4. Your Causal Signature & the Blueprint of Abundance

Every soul carries a **causal signature**—a unique vibrational pattern encoded in the higher planes.
That signature determines how wealth, power, and influence flow through you.

When your life is built in harmony with that signature, wealth flows.
When you abandon that signature to survive, fit in, or imitate others, the field collapses.

This is why copying others never works.
Because your causal blueprint is non-transferable.

To activate it, ask:

- What feels most naturally abundant in me?

- What do I magnetize when I'm not trying?

- Where do others receive transformation through me—without effort?

- What environments expand my signal?

These questions bring you back into **alignment with your divine function**. And when you align with your function, wealth is not optional—it is **magnetically inevitable**.

Summary:

- Wealth is more than manifestation—it is remembrance.

- Spiritual assets live in the causal body and precede material effort.

- Access requires energetic alignment, not hustle.

- Your field must broadcast permission before wealth will arrive.

THE ARCHITECTURE OF WEALTH – LECTURE V

The Time Illusion, False Timelines & Instant Manifestation Windows

At the metaphysical level, time is not a neutral container.
It is a **construct that shapes belief**, and therefore, shapes access.

When it comes to wealth, most people unconsciously enter into **linear agreements**:

- "It'll take years to build security."
- "Wealth only comes through long, hard effort."
- "Step-by-step is the only safe path."
- "It's not my time yet."

These are not just thoughts.
They are **contractual time-loops**—energetic sequences that push manifestation into the future indefinitely.

You do not just delay your wealth—you architect its distance.

1. Linear Thinking as an Energetic Delay Mechanism

Linear thinking is a product of the lower mind. It processes reality as **cause → effect**, chained through time.

While this has utility in practical life, it **becomes a trap** when applied to quantum manifestation.

Why?

Because in the metaphysical system of wealth, manifestation is not chronological—it is **frequency-based**.

Reality does not respond to what stage you're in.
It responds to what **field you are broadcasting right now**.

You don't have to climb steps.
You need to collapse the timeline entirely—and **step into a vibrational now** where the frequency of wealth already exists.

This is how certain souls "quantum leap"—they don't skip steps; they dissolve them.

2. Time Loops as Self-Sabotaging Architectures

A time loop is a **self-protective belief** designed to delay confrontation with abundance.

Examples:

- "Let me prepare first."
- "Let me heal first."
- "I'll be ready once I finish these trainings."
- "I just need more time to get clear."

Each of these creates a **looped horizon**—wealth is always just beyond the next hill. Never here. Never now.

What's the deeper reason?

Most often: guilt, unworthiness, or subconscious fear of expansion.

So instead of saying "I'm afraid to receive," we say "it's not the right time."

But wealth only arrives when you **occupy the version of yourself** that can receive it fully in the present moment.

That version is not in the future.
It is **stored in a higher field**, accessible through collapse—not delay.

3. Instant Manifestation Windows: Accessing Nonlinear Frequency Points

There are moments—windows—where your inner and outer fields align so precisely that manifestation can happen instantly.

These windows don't operate on time.
They operate on **total coherence** between:

- Belief
- Readiness
- Frequency
- Environment

- Archetypal alignment

You don't create these moments.
You **enter** them—by withdrawing all energy from false timelines and returning to the core signal of your soul.

When you do this, time bends.
Reality shifts.
Wealth appears—not because it "arrived," but because your field finally stopped resisting its presence.

4. Dissolving Time Agreements

Ask yourself:

- What future date am I unconsciously waiting for?

- What inner rules have I created that delay my abundance?

- Who taught me that wealth must be slow, hard, or earned through exhaustion?

- What belief would I have to hold for wealth to arrive now?

Lecture V *Collapsing the timeline*

Then declare:

"I collapse the illusion of linear time. I revoke all false timelines and choose present-field alignment with abundance."

"I no longer delay. I no longer prepare. I AM the version that receives now."

This is not bypassing.
This is energetic sovereignty.

Summary:

- Time is not neutral—it is often an encoded delay mechanism.

- Wealth does not require sequence. It requires frequency.

- Instant manifestation is not magic—it is structural alignment with your higher self.

- You must dissolve your time-based conditions and step into *field coherence* now.

THE ARCHITECTURE OF WEALTH – LECTURE VI

Energetic Exchange, Value Fields & the Law of Resonant Return

Wealth is not "earned" in the way most people believe.
In metaphysics, wealth is not payment—it is **reflection**.
A mirror response to the **value frequency you emit into the grid of others.**

This principle is known as the **Law of Resonant Return**.

You do not get what you *want*.
You do not get what you *need*.
You receive what you *radiate*—based on the value you circulate into the consciousness field around you.

If your field emits incoherence, doubt, or fragmentation,
you break the circuit of return.
If your field emits coherence, clarity, and service-aligned power,
return is not optional—it is **structurally inevitable.**

Lecture VI   *Resonant return*

1. Value Is Frequency, Not Function

In the physical world, value is measured in units: skills, credentials, hours.
But in metaphysical reality, **value is measured in coherence**.

Coherence means that your inner frequency is fully aligned with what you offer.
There is no distortion, no guilt, no posturing, no scarcity.

When you are coherent, others feel it—not just as confidence, but as a kind of **energetic infrastructure**.
They trust your field.
They invest in your signal.

This is why two people can offer the same service—
and one magnetizes effortlessly, while the other repels.

It's not about the offer.
It's about the **signal** behind it.

2. The Mechanics of Resonant Return

Everything you project enters a field of exchange.

- If you emit value with distortion (neediness, guilt, pressure), the return is delayed or denied.

- If you emit value with purity and clarity, the field **echoes** your frequency back through money, opportunity, relationships, or support.

This return is not dependent on one person.
It is not linear.
You can give in one place and receive from ten others.

The field doesn't pay you.
The field reflects you.

3. Scarcity Fields: Breaking the Circuit

When you withhold your gifts, delay your offerings, or underprice your value due to

Lecture VI   *Resonant return*

internal fragmentation, you are sending this message to the field:

"I do not believe what I carry has enough worth."

And the field answers:

"Then we shall not return it."

This isn't punishment.
It is **resonance**.

Your field is always respected.
If it says "I am unsure," the grid reflects uncertainty.
If it says "I am unworthy," the grid responds with rejection.

Scarcity is not about what's missing.
It's about what you are refusing to emit.

4. Wealth Is the Echo of What You've Given Without Distortion

The field remembers every transmission.
Every moment you gave from soul-aligned power...
Every time your offering was clean, clear, and undistorted by survival...

Those frequencies circulate.
They travel.
They gather momentum.

Eventually, they return.
Not always how you expect.
But always in harmony with the signal you emitted.

The mistake most people make is trying to *get* before they *radiate*.

But the secret is:

Emit coherence, and return becomes unavoidable.

Summary:

- Value is not based on effort. It is based on frequency.

- Your energetic field is your currency.

- The Law of Resonant Return ensures that what you emit into the field—when coherent—**always returns**.

- To unlock wealth, radiate value **without distortion**.

THE ARCHITECTURE OF WEALTH – LECTURE VII

Field Sovereignty: Sealing Your Wealth Grid from Interference and Leakage

Sovereignty is not control. It is not domination.
Sovereignty is the **energetic authority** to govern your own signal—without unconscious leakage, dependency, or distortion.

In wealth manifestation, sovereignty is the final architecture.
It is the **container** that holds all previous alignments—belief, coherence, resonance, causality—and keeps them from fragmenting under pressure.

You cannot attract true wealth without sovereignty.
Because until your field is sealed, it is **vulnerable to outside charge**—to others' guilt, shame, scarcity, projections, and spiritual manipulation.

1. What Is Field Leakage?

Field leakage is the **unconscious dispersion of your energy** into people, systems, or thought-forms that are not aligned with your wealth grid.

It happens through:

- People-pleasing
- Over-explaining your worth
- Holding guilt for receiving
- Internalized rejection from past betrayals
- Sharing your vision with unworthy ears
- Accepting energetic contracts of obligation disguised as loyalty

Every leak creates an **energetic vulnerability**.
And wealth does not pour into unsealed vessels.

Lecture VII *Field Sovereignty*

2. The Spiritual Cost of Energetic Dependency

Most people are not sovereign.
They operate in a **borrowed field**—where their sense of worth and power is tied to external validation, relationships, or perceived acceptance.

This creates a constant drain.
You may build wealth temporarily, but it slips through the cracks of your dependencies.

Signs of dependency:

- Needing others to "see" your greatness

- Holding back until you're validated

- Shrinking when misunderstood

- Financial collapse after rejection or abandonment

These are not financial issues.
They are **sovereignty fractures**.

3. Sovereignty as Energetic Insulation

To become sovereign is to **seal the field**.

You no longer seek permission.
You no longer collapse to external frequency.
You no longer confuse reaction with resonance.

A sovereign field has these traits:

- Internal certainty independent of external agreement

- Zero tolerance for energetic disrespect

- Capacity to receive and retain wealth without explanation

- Refusal to over-serve, undercharge, or self-abandon

- Clear edges: what enters, what stays out, what feeds, what drains

4. Sealing the Wealth Grid: The Ritual of Completion

Every energetic leak is a **contract**—some old, some ancestral.
To close them, you must complete the agreements you never knew you made.

Say aloud:

"I revoke all unconscious contracts that bind my wealth to others' permission, pain, or perception."
"I withdraw all energy I gave out of guilt, need, or fear of rejection."
"I seal my field. I radiate from source. I operate in sovereign abundance."
"I owe no one my light. I share it by choice, not obligation."

This declaration isn't just symbolic—it reorganizes your grid.
It closes loops.
Ends siphons.
Returns power.

Summary:

- Sovereignty is the container of your wealth. Without it, manifestation collapses under pressure.

- Field leakage occurs when you invest energy in external approval or unhealed loyalty.

- Wealth retention requires insulation, boundaries, and withdrawal from all unconscious contracts.

- Sovereignty is the gateway to sustained abundance—without depletion.

You now carry the full system.

But this is only the beginning. Each of these seven lectures is a door—
A gate into deeper layers of the **inner architecture of wealth**.

From this point forward, you are no longer "attracting" wealth.
You are **emitting** the blueprint that makes it inevitable.

THE ARCHITECTURE OF WEALTH – ADVANCED TRANSMISSION I

Wealth as a Weapon of Consciousness

Wealth, in its purest metaphysical form, is not comfort.
It is **capacity**.
A weapon—not of aggression, but of leverage. Of accelerated force applied to reality.

In the hands of the sovereign, wealth becomes an instrument of **liberation**—a way to amplify truth, reorganize power, and dismantle the false constructs built on fear, dependence, and deprivation.

1. Wealth Multiplies Whatever Consciousness Holds It

Wealth does not change people.
It **reveals** them.
And it **magnifies** them.

Whatever your frequency is—wealth will expand it.

- If you are fragmented, wealth increases chaos.

- If you are whole, wealth increases power.

- If you are aligned, wealth increases influence.

Wealth is **neutral until directed**—then it becomes weaponized through the intention of its holder.

This is why spiritual beings must reclaim wealth—not as an attachment, but as a **force of alignment**.

2. The Soul's Use of Wealth in the Great Game of Consciousness

You are not here to "survive."
You are here to **anchor blueprints**.
To construct realities. To shift timelines. To redistribute light.

And in this current dimensional grid, wealth is one of the most potent vectors of impact.

When held consciously:

- It collapses false hierarchies.
- It funds divine rebellion.
- It destabilizes old control systems.
- It frees your energy from maintenance to mastery.

When wealth is in the hands of aligned consciousness, the grid must adapt.
Entire systems bend.

This is why so many awakened souls have been subconsciously programmed to reject wealth—because their full access would **disrupt too much**.

But now the contract has changed.

You are no longer here to *avoid* power.
You are here to **restructure** it.

3. Money Is Not Evil—It Is Amplification

The idea that money corrupts is only true if the field is already corrupt.
In truth, money is **an amplifier of signal**.

In your hands, it is not greed.
It is geometry.

It becomes a frequency weapon—directed by your will to create sovereign infrastructures, heal karmic dislocation, and fund light into matter.

To fear wealth is to fear your own expansion.

4. The Metaphysical Reclamation of Wealth as Power

Say aloud:

"I reclaim wealth as a tool of consciousness."
"I no longer fear the responsibility of power."

"I direct energy without guilt, delay, or apology."
"I do not worship wealth. I weaponize it—to build the new."

Summary:

- Wealth amplifies what already exists within the holder.

- In awakened hands, wealth becomes a frequency weapon to collapse false structures and expand new systems.

- Reclaiming wealth is not a selfish act —it is a **strategic alignment with your function in the grid**.

- You are not here to chase comfort. You are here to command structure.

THE ARCHITECTURE OF WEALTH – ADVANCED TRANSMISSION II

The Alchemy of Circulation

Wealth is not meant to be held.
It is meant to **circulate.**

To move is to remain alive.
To stagnate is to collapse into decay.

Wealth is not defined by how much you *possess*, but by how efficiently and intelligently you **channel flow**.

This is not economics.
This is **alchemy**.

1. Circulation as Energetic Breath

Just as the lungs inhale and exhale, your wealth field must **receive and release** in rhythm.
When you hoard, undercharge, or restrict your giving out of fear or control, you disrupt the current.

- **Overgiving** leads to depletion.
- **Undergiving** leads to stagnation.
- **Overholding** leads to field suffocation.
- **Undercharging** leads to erosion of signal.

In true alchemy, circulation is **conscious movement of power**—strategic outflow with magnetic inflow.

The question is never "How much do I keep?"
It's "What current is my field meant to direct right now?"

2. The Consequences of Energetic Hoarding

Money, energy, attention, opportunity—when these are **held out of fear**, you enter what is known as **energetic contraction**.

Your field begins to shrink.
Your aura tightens.
Your magnetism drops.
The grid stops responding.

You don't attract because you've signaled lack.

Hoarding is not safety. It is a death spiral. It breaks the resonance that creates return.

Wealth is a river.
It does not bless the stagnant.

3. Charging, Receiving, and the Magnetism of Equal Exchange

To undercharge is to betray your field.

When you give high-frequency transmissions, products, services, or presence—and receive less than the field's resonance—**you create a frequency imbalance.**

That imbalance begins to fragment your sovereignty.

You weaken yourself every time you accept less than your field deserves.

This is not about greed. It's about **field integrity**.

If you give 10 and receive 2,
you train the field that your signal is optional.
Eventually, the return ceases entirely.

The true alchemist is not afraid to receive in full.
Because they know: receiving is **retention of current**.
And only retained current can build momentum.

4. Circulatory Consciousness: Activating the Current

Wealth comes when you prove to the grid that you can **move energy cleanly.**
Not hoard it.
Not waste it.
Not abandon yourself in the process.

You must become a **conscious circuit** of wealth—where the inflow matches the outflow, and the entire system is designed to amplify the whole.

Say aloud:

"I am a living current of wealth."
"I do not hoard. I circulate power with intelligence and clarity."
"I receive in full. I give in alignment. I build flow, not stagnation."
"My wealth field breathes, moves, and amplifies."

Summary:

- Circulation is the breath of wealth.

- Hoarding or undercharging weakens your magnetic field.

- Conscious outflow matched with clear inflow maintains field strength and sovereign power.

- You are not a container of wealth—you are a **conductor** of it.

THE ARCHITECTURE OF WEALTH – ADVANCED TRANSMISSION III

The Geometry of Divine Compensation

Nothing is ever lost.
In the architecture of higher law, **energy is never wasted**, only reallocated.
Wealth operates on a principle far beyond fairness—it obeys a deeper law: **harmonic compensation**.

This is the law that governs your field across lifetimes.
Everything you've given in alignment—
whether seen, honored, or forgotten—
remains encoded in your soul's vault.

This law ensures:

You are always compensated— precisely, geometrically, energetically —for what you truly emit.

1. Compensation Is Not Immediate. It Is Harmonically Timed

Wealth does not always return on your timeline.
It returns on your **frequency readiness**.

You may have planted seeds years ago—in relationships, in service, in truth—but if your field wasn't yet coherent enough to receive the return, it was delayed.

Delayed is not denied.
The law of divine compensation stores those frequencies until **your field stabilizes into the version of you that can hold the reward without collapse.**

Once that version is embodied, return becomes automatic.

2. Nothing Is Wasted—But Much Is Redirected

When you give from guilt, need, or self-abandonment,
the field still receives the charge—but it is **redirected**.

That energy doesn't disappear. It simply returns to you in distorted forms:

- Exhaustion
- Confusion
- Passive resistance
- Invisible self-worth erosion
- Lessons in boundaries

The law is precise, not sentimental.

You will always be repaid—in clarity or in correction.

3. The Architecture of the Return: Why You Are Repaid in Form, Not Always in Currency

You may expect money, but the field returns wealth in **the form you most need** to advance your soul architecture.

If you gave love, you may be returned opportunity.

If you gave clarity, you may be returned influence.

If you gave vision, you may be returned relationships, territory, or momentum.

Currency is only one mode of compensation. The **real currency is evolution.**

And the field always prioritizes your next frequency over your current preference.

4. Activating the Law: Conscious Claiming Without Entitlement

This law cannot be forced. But it can be **activated** through conscious reclamation.

Say aloud:

"I trust the field to repay every frequency I've ever transmitted in truth."
"Nothing I've given is lost. It is stored, multiplied, and returned in harmonic precision."
"I claim full alignment with the return of my spiritual, emotional, and energetic investments."

"I receive not from effort—but from field integrity."

This is not entitlement.
It is **recognition** of the law.

You are not begging for return.
You are **recalibrating to receive it.**

Final Summary:

- Wealth is governed by the law of divine compensation—what you emit in truth always returns.

- Returns may be delayed until your field can hold them.

- Compensation is not always financial—it is energetic, structural, and evolutionary.

- You must become the vessel strong enough to hold the harmonic return.

Ancient The Architect

THE BENEDICTION OF SOVEREIGN WEALTH

A Closing Transmission to Seal the Grid

I now withdraw all projections of lack, all timelines of delay, all ancestral permissions for poverty.
I collapse every field that was built on fear, on guilt, on struggle, or survival.

I reclaim wealth—not as a possession, but as a field of power.
Not as an escape, but as a structure.
Not as a hope, but as a function of who I am.

Every distortion is returned to source.
Every leak is sealed.
Every contract not aligned with my sovereign self is revoked.

I do not chase wealth.
I *radiate it*.

I do not beg.
I *transmit*.

I do not bargain.
I *architect*.

Wealth comes not because I want it.
It comes because I have aligned with the law that governs its return.

I am not the seeker of gold.
I am the keeper of the field.
And from this field flows all that is needed—without struggle, without shame, without collapse.

I activate every dormant treasury in my causal body.
I awaken the soul codes of abundance.
I allow divine compensation to flood my field—now, without delay, without distortion, without apology.

May my wealth be clean.
May it be precise.
May it be used in service of the Great Alignment.

This is the benediction.
This is the seal.
This is the end of delay.

It is done.

www.ingramcontent.com/pod-product-compliance
Lightning Source LLC
Chambersburg PA
CBHW071514150426
43191CB00009B/1526